How To Live On An Island

by Sandy Gingras

DOWN
THE
SHORE
PUBLISHING

Down The Shore Publishing Corp., Box 100, West Creek, NJ 08092
www.down-the-shore.com

The words "Down The Shore" and the Down The Shore Publishing logo are a registered U.S. Trademark.

Revised hardcover edition, 1998
First published, 1996 in a trade paper edition (ISBN 0-945582-32-3).
Printed in China.
10 9 8

Library of Congress Cataloging-in-Publication Data
    Gingras, Sandy, 1958-
        How to live on an island / by Sandy Gingras.
            p.   cm. -- (A cormorant book)
        ISBN 0-945582-32-3 (pbk)
        ISBN 0-945582-57-9 (hc)
        1. Aphorisms and apothegms. 2. Islands -- Quotations, maxims, etc.
    I. Title. II. Series
    PN6278.168G56   1996
    741.5'973--dc20   95-19956
                            CIP

ISBN-13   978-0-945582-57-1

for morgAn

How To Live On An ISLAnd

I think that there's no truer place than an island. Whether it's a sandbar or a bubble-up of volcanic rock or a jut of tropical coral, an island stands only by some whim of fate, given a chancy foothold among the chaos. When I go to an island, I know that I'm in that state of grace in which anything can happen.

oops

There's an island near where I live that keeps disappearing under water and then appearing again every few decades. People can't resist it. They go to picnic on it, dance on it, drink to it. They want to claim it as their own--in all of its fleeting improbability. I like to go out there and just stand on it. It almost convinces me that there is such a place as the present.

My son (who is eight) says that islands are places where you change a lot (he means bathing suits). But living on an island often makes you change your sense of perspective, your mind and your direction too. With the tide coming in over the castles you build, the currents sweeping you places you didn't plan on going, the mists rolling in mysteriously over what you thought was clear, you change a lot just to keep up.

"a couple changes of heart too..."

Islands can be scary places, but their changeability makes them hopeful places too. Each day starts washed, swept, utterly different than the day before. The morning crackles like a never-turned page. Where else in the world do we get the chance to step out into so much renewal? Where else do we keep getting second chances at ourselves?

snap crackle
hope
another new page

A day on an island can be like a ride on a wild thing. The ground shifts and hisses, the boundaries grow and recede. The tides yearn. The moon pulls. The very air pushes us around. I can't help but know that a day here is not that grounded predictable thing I thought (sometimes hoped) it was, but it's as swervy and alive as we are.

... the moon PULLS

It's not always easy to live on an island. There's not only a geographical but an emotional distance between isolation and connection. I've become better at making the trip back and forth. I used to be afraid of bridges. Now I know that every bridge is a kind of heart, with its own reach and try, its own need for support. I've come to love ferries and trust the stubborn chug of them.

the stubborn chug

And I've learned to love the view from in between.

Sometimes life seems like a hurricane hurrying us and swirling us along too fast. An island, for me, is a still point. It's like the eye of the hurricane, except an island's eye is lazy... probably closed, taking a nap in the sun, letting life just sink in. An island never lets us forget the great value of doing nothing.

Sink in...
z z z z z z z...
sink sink o o o

how To Live

sunburn Trouble spot

Many people live or vacation on islands because they're in search of a simpler life.

But sometimes the trip to simplicity becomes a complicated one -- just think of what most people pack! And it's often a long journey (especially with traffic). What always helped me as a kid when we were going on summer vacation was rolling the windows down. Then I'd notice everything I could see, and I'd just breathe. These things still help me to get to simplicity. If you're going, maybe they'll help you too...

The main road

To simplicity

heavy air

reduce speed

be Transported

fLOAT

make a Splash

LISTen in on SheLLS

stretch

run with waves

Laugh Like A Gull

CARRY A bucket

BOOGIE

Sugar yourself with sand

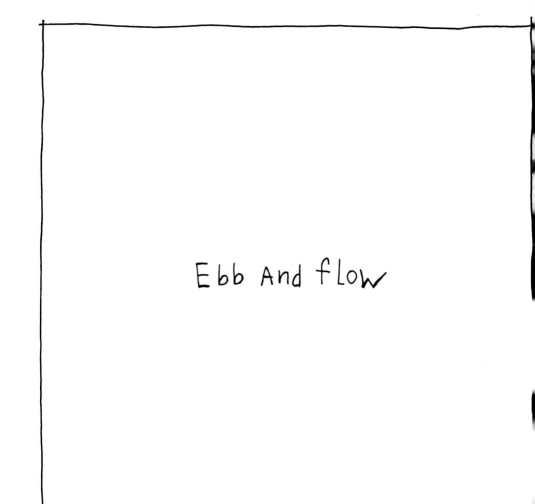

Ebb And flow

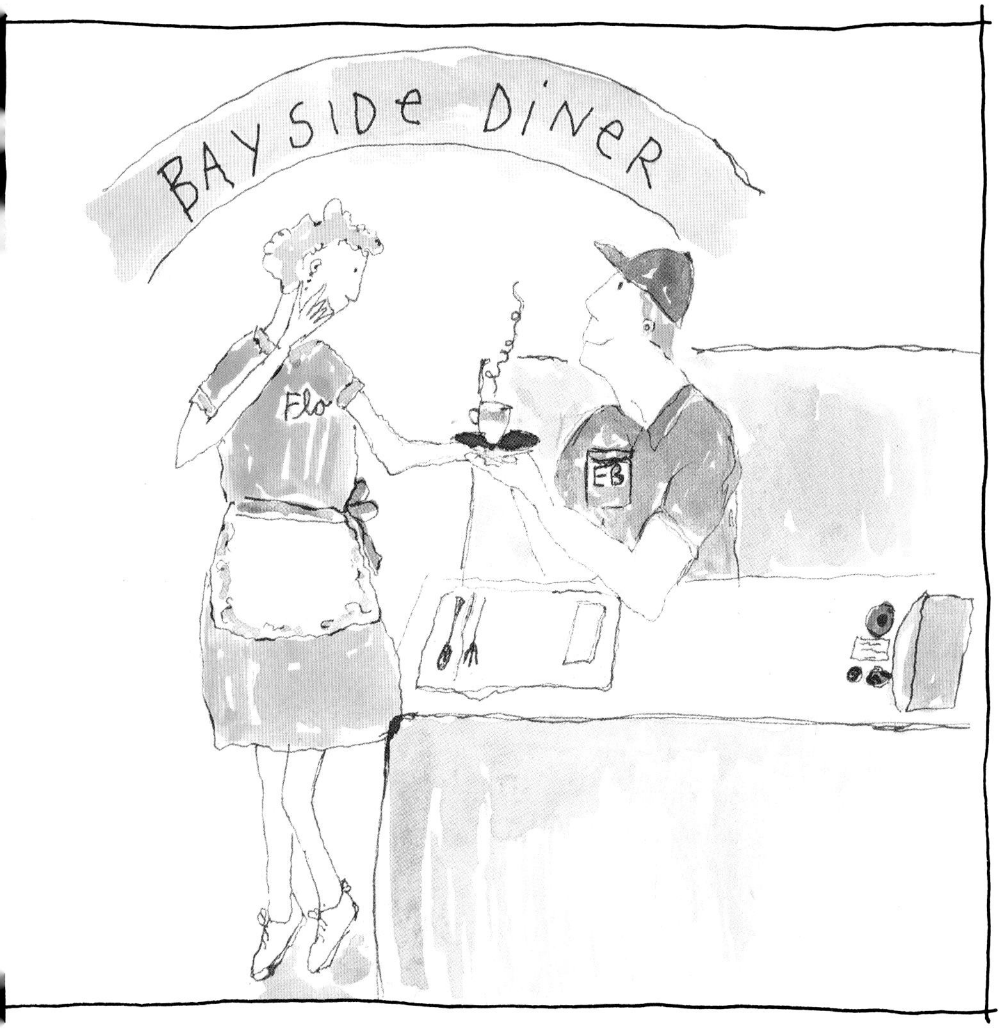
BAYSIDE DINER
Flo
EB

ride rusty bikes--
Go with the wind

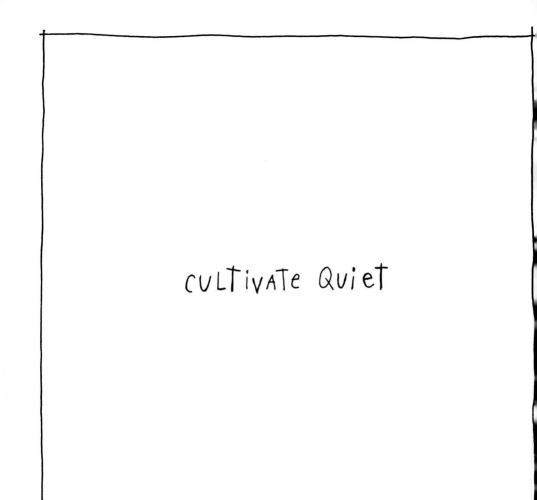

CULTiVATe QUieT

tune up your senses

WALK Tender

put Living Things back

dANCe on edGes

build CASTLeS And LeAVe
them for The moon
To find

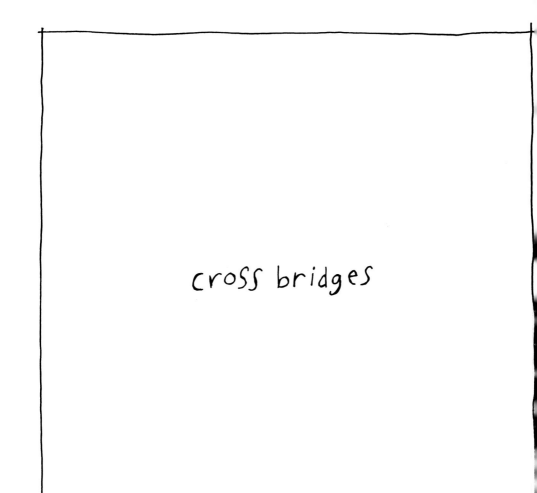

cross bridges

discover TreAsure

THANK

About the Author

Sandy Gingras is an artist and writer with her own design company called "How To Live" (visit her website at www.how-to-live.com). She and her son and two cats live near the beach on an island in New Jersey, where she is active in efforts to preserve open space and wetlands.

If you liked this book, you'll also enjoy these other books by Sandy Gingras:

Reasons to be Happy at the Beach
ISBN 0-945582-98-6

"Happiness is all around us. We are looking at it, breathing it, holding it in our hands."

How to Live at the Beach
ISBN 0-945582-73-0

"Like the ocean itself, this book nourishes the mind, heart, and soul."

— Coastal Living Magazine

At the Beach House - A Guest Book
ISBN 1-59322-006-5

A great way to remember all your visitors with sandy feet.

In a House by the Sea
ISBN 1-59322-013-8

"A reminder that happiness and the beach go hand in hand."

— Publishers Weekly

The Uh-oh Heart
ISBN 0-945582-96-X

For all of us with uh-oh hearts fearful of growing and risking and loving.

How to be a Friend
ISBN 0-945582-99-4

A little book that celebrates friendship.

Down The Shore Publishing offers other book and calendar titles (with a special emphasis on the coast). For a free catalog, or to be added to our mailing list, just send us a request.

Down The Shore Publishing
P.O. Box 100 ❖ West Creek, NJ 08092
or email: info@down-the-shore.com
www.down-the-shore.com